THE OFFICIAL LEGO® NINJAGO™ ANNUAL 2016

CONTENTS

GUARDING NINJAGO

The Overlord has been trying to take over Ninjago for a long time, and only the Spinjitzu Masters can stand up to him. Their last battle ended with the young ninja's victory, but it came at a great price. One of the warriors, Zane, sacrificed himself to defeat the evil Overlord.

The young Ninja of Fire, Earth, Lightning and Creation have received an invitation to Master Chen's mysterious island, where a Tournament of Elements is to take place. Will visiting the island help them discover what happened to their lost friend?

After defeating the evil Overlord, the group went their separate ways. The Green Ninja stayed behind, remaining faithful to the ideals of Spinjitzu. Now it is time to reunite the young masters. Help Lloyd find his way to the other three ninja. Lead them out of the labyrinth together.

START

FINISH

THE TEAM REUNITED

Kai, Jay, Cole and Lloyd are students of Sensei Wu and his brother, Sensei Garmadon. Each of them wields a different element. Although they have very different personalities and abilities, as a team they are inseparable. Let's get to know these amazing fighters a little better.

LLOYD

Lloyd was the only ninja to continue training under the watchful eye of his father, Sensei Garmadon. He managed to bring the team back together and convince the young warriors to keep searching for Zane. Despite being the youngest ninja, Lloyd is the one to renew the team's strength.

COLE

When Zane disappeared, the Ninja of Earth hid his true identity and became a lumberjack, seeking peace in a remote forest.
Now he's back, stronger and more determined than ever, and he must prove once again that he is the rock of the ninja team.

KAI

Although still impatient and combative, Kai is now much better at controlling his inner fire. After the team split he spent his time competing in masked duels in Ninjago's shady bars. He doesn't know it yet, but a great adventure and great love await him ...

JAY

After leaving the group, the Ninja of Lightning went on to host a television show. Being a famous TV star suited Jay just fine, but he couldn't forget his missing friend, so he quit the celebrity lifestyle and reunited with the team to help find Zane.

ZANE

What exactly happened to Zane? He sacrificed himself to save Ninjago, but is he really gone forever? Or is it possible that Zane is still alive? Perhaps his best friends can find the answers to these questions on Master Chen's mysterious island ...

MASTER CHEN

Who is the mysterious Master Chen? To find the truth, count the snake symbols on each card. The card with the most symbols holds the correct answer.

1. He is the famous organiser of tournaments and trips on far-away islands, a seasoned guide on serpentine tracks, and a connoisseur of homemade noodles.

2. A well-known snake enthusiast and snake rights defender, he started the foundation "Ana can do". It is rumoured that he likes his snake friends better than people.

3. Officially, he is the owner of the Noodle Empire. Unofficially, he's the leader of the Anacondrai cult. The Snake tribe's aim is to rule the world.

4. He is an eccentric millionaire who has a secret alter ego. At night, Chen puts on a costume made from snake's skin and slithers along the streets of the city to fight crime!

Master Chen used to be Sensei
Garmadon's teacher.

SERVANTS OF THE NOODLE KING

Throughout the years, Master Chen has recruited many dangerous crooks into his loyal army. The warriors in rows A, B and C are lining up for battle. Figure out the patterns and write the number of the crook that should come next in each row.

THE CHASE

During a spying mission on Master Chen's island, Kai came across a group of Chen's fierce guards. One of the guards spotted the ninja and ran after him into the trees!

Gotta dash! I'll go this way!

He's still behind me! If I don't lose him, I'll have to fight him!

HA!

See you at the finish line!

MECH STRIKES BACK

Jay, the Ninja of Lightning, is a tough fighter in a league of his own. When he's behind the controls of his Mech, he's unstoppable. Look closely at the five pictures of Jay's powerful machine and circle the two pictures that are exactly the same.

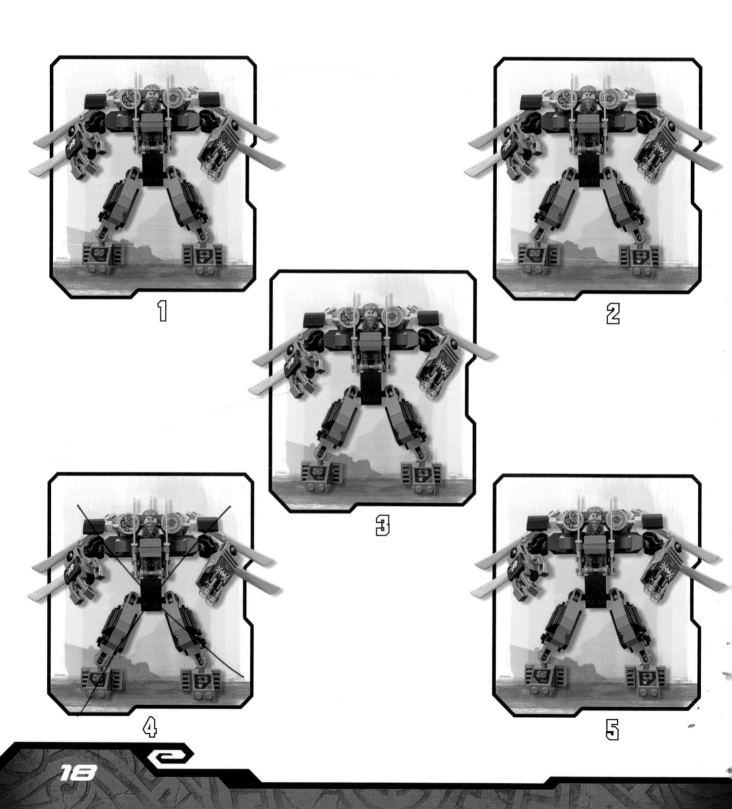

1

2

3

4

5

IN THE NET

Kai is trapped. Help him free himself from the net! How many times can you see the word SPINJITZU? Find them all, then Kai can use his power to break loose.

WHO'S WHO?

The ninja are taught that to defeat your enemies, you must get to know them first. Look closely at the portraits of Chen's thugs and match them with the right descriptions.

Like every other guard in Chen's army, he loves tattoos. But this guard is different than the others because he is a master with an axe. (A)

1
ZUGU

2
EYEZOR

He is the chief of Master Chen's prison. His fanged shoulder pads are red and his sword is incredibly sharp. (B)

He dreams of performing evil deeds, but never actually does them. He thinks that wearing one red sleeve makes him look especially fierce. (C)

3
SLEVEN

4 KAPAU

This one likes to brag that he's the best fighter. The truth is, in battle, he usually trips on his spear.

D

Chen's most trusted thug. Bad to the bone. He has one eye and spiky hair.

E

5 KRAIT

6 CHOPE

This evil warrior likes to scare his opponents with a weapon that looks like a snake fang.

F

KRAIT'S STYLE

Krait wants a tough car that shows off his might. He's putting rims on his tyres to match his tattoos! Which tyres does he choose to soup-up the Anacondrai Crusher? Find the rim that matches the one he's already put on the car.

Did you know?

There are two launchers hidden in the front of Krait's vehicle that shoot poison darts.

FIERY STORIES

Did you know?

Master Chen's warriors want only one thing - to turn into powerful Anacondrai Snakes.

This is a part of the Legend of the Spinjitzu Masters.
Which fragment best describes the scene?

"The Blue Ninja has lightning reflexes that help him avoid the trap and attack the enemy."

A

"The sneaky villain opened the trap door under Cole, but at the last moment the Ninja of Earth launched himself at the thug and soared past the pit."

C

"Master Chen`s warrior knocked the weapon from Kai`s hands and disarmed the helpless ninja on the bridge."

B

MASTER OF SPEED

Is it a bird? No. Is it an arrow? Definitely not. It's Griffin Turner! Find out if you are faster than the Master of Speed. You have 45 seconds to count all the weapons and write the numbers in the correct boxes. Test your reflexes! Set a stopwatch! And ... go!

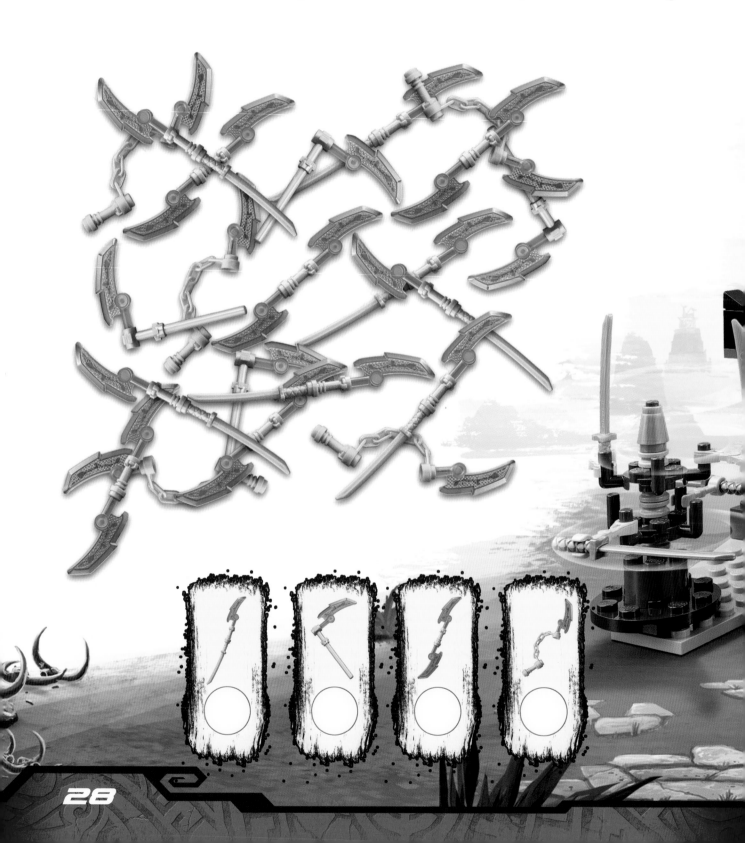

Griffin Turner is the record holder for all running sports events in Ninjago.

JUNGLE MAZE

Jay has caught one of Chen's thugs and is on his way to interrogate him. Suddenly, members of the vicious Anacondrai cult are after him! He needs your help. Lead the ninja safely through the thick jungle. Hurry!

FINISH

START

A DANGEROUS BEAUTY

Skylor's amazing copycat skills make her a very dangerous foe. She can steal elemental powers simply by touching a master. Look closely at the shadows and circle the one that belongs to this mighty warrior.

Did you know?

Skylor stole Kai's heart when they first met aboard the ship that carried them to Master Chen's island ...

LOST WEAPONS

The Masters of the Elements are not the Masters of Tidying Up. Help the warriors count how many weapons were left outside all night then write the total in the box next to each weapon.

3

1

3

2

ROUGH RIDE

The Anacondrai Crusher's double rotor with triple blades is ready to attack, and the ninja must disable it quickly! Which ninja gets there first?

Master Chen's thugs like the Anacondrai so much that even their vehicles have a snake-like look.

A SPECIAL TASK

Deep down in the dark tunnels of Master Chen's fortress ...

I'm telling you, Master Chen thinks highly of our service.

Otherwise, he wouldn't have given us this important task.

Well ...

He must have seen me doing my ...

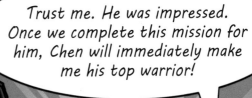

WORST IDEA EVER

Did you know?

Kai was tempted to join Master Chen's ranks, but he remained loyal to his friends.

One of Chen's men attacked Kai in the jungle. He'll never do that again! Look at the fragments and mark the ones that don't appear in the picture with a cross.

STEEL-HANDED MASTER

Karlof – the Master of Steel – is from distant Metalonia. He may not look very smart, but he's actually a genius. Karlof can do this sudoku puzzle in less than twenty seconds. How long will it take you? Complete the grid by drawing the missing pictures, but remember that the same weapon cannot appear twice in any row or column. Ready, steady ... GO!

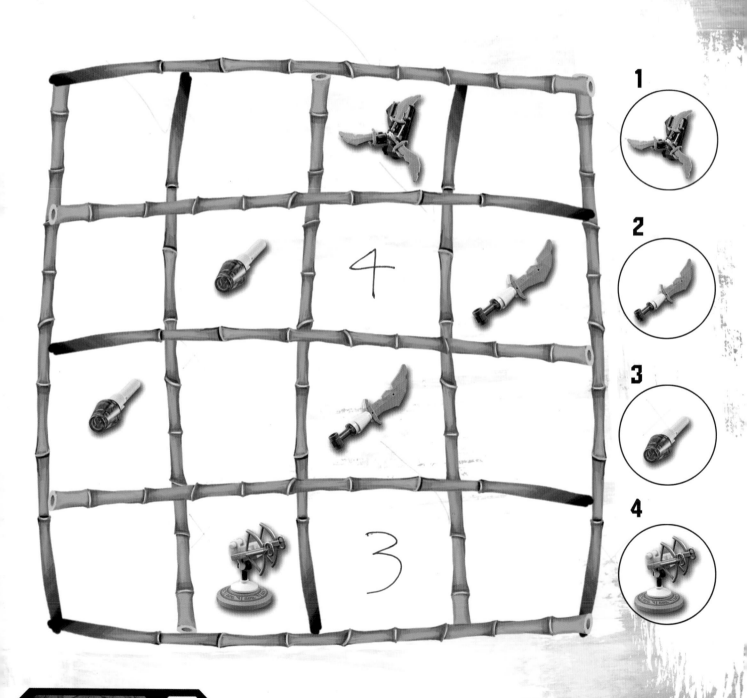

Karlof can turn his body into hard steel for about two minutes.

ANCIENT LABYRINTH

A clever ninja knows when to fight and when to retreat. Lloyd hid in the ruins of a prehistoric temple to avoid great danger. Now he needs your help to get out of there!

FINISH

Did you know?

Lloyd drives a vehicle built by Kai's sister, Nya.

START

The Masters of Elements snuck into Master Chen's dojo to steal some weapons, but he discovered their plan! The elemental warriors need to escape, quickly. Find five differences between these two pictures and mark them clearly so they can get out of there.

2

TARGET PRACTICE

Cole is searching for the last few members of Chen's guard, but the enemies are hiding! Find all the evil warriors and circle them so that the ninja can chase them away.

GHOSTLY GUESTS

Master Chen and his followers fell through a portal. Unfortunately, the same portal let some dangerous spirits into our world! Match the shadows with the unwelcome guests.

MORRO'S GHOST

A long time ago, Morro was Sensei Wu's first pupil. He was in training to be the Green Ninja, but there was a darkness inside him and a thirst for absolute power. Look at the picture of Morro below, then find the same picture in the lineup opposite.

THE POSSESSION OF LLOYD

Evil Morro possessed Lloyd's body and now he's bringing a great dragon to attack Ninjago. The ninja warriors are already on his tail. Match the fragments with the missing spaces in this amazing battle scene.

AIR BATTLE

The young ninjas are ready for a counterattack. It's time to banish the ghosts from Ninjago forever! Look at the picture and circle the portraits of the warriors who don't appear in the battle.

ANSWERS

PAGE 9
GREEN NINJA'S MISSION

START

FINISH

PAGE 12
MASTER CHEN

3. Officially, he is the owner of the Noodle Empire. Unofficially, he's the leader of the Anacondrai cult. The Snake tribe's aim is to rule the world.

PAGE 15
SERVANTS OF THE NOODLE KING

A — 3
B — 2
C — 5

PAGE 18
MECH STRIKES BACK

 1

 5

PAGE 20
IN THE NET

PAGES 22-23
WHO'S WHO?

A – 5, B – 1, C – 4,
D – 6, E – 2, F – 3.

PAGE 27
FIERY STORIES

C

PAGE 28
MASTER OF SPEED

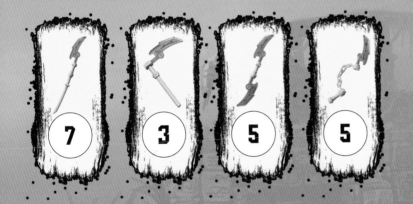

7   3   5   5

PAGE 32
A DANGEROUS BEAUTY

5

PAGE 24
KRAIT'S STYLE

4

PAGE 31
JUNGLE MAZE

FINISH

START

PAGE 35
LOST WEAPONS

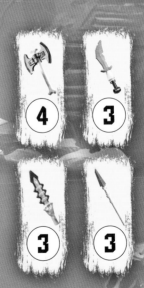

4   3

3   3

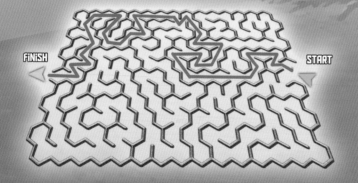

HOW TO BUILD COLE